LOVELAND PUBLIC LIBRARY

S0-AUJ-005

1130005
$18.60
I
JNF

Hoaxes, Fibs, and Fakes

Lisa Thompson

CHELSEA HOUSE
PUBLISHERS
A Haights Cross Communications ✦ Company ®

This hard cover edition first published in 2005
by Chelsea House Publishers

Copyright © 2003 Sundance Publishing

This edition of The Real Deal is published
by arrangement with Blake Education.
All rights reserved. No part of this publication
may be reproduced or transmitted in any form
or by any means, electronic or mechanical,
including photocopy, recording, or any
information or retrieval system, without
permission in writing from the publisher.

Published by
Sundance Publishing
P.O. Box 740
One Beeman Road
Northborough, MA 01532–0740
800-343-8204
www.sundancepub.com

Copyright © text Lisa Thompson
Copyright © illustrations Lloyd Foye and Cliff Watt

First published 2002 by
Blake Education, Locked Bag 2022, Glebe 2037, Australia
Exclusive United States Distribution: Sundance Publishing

Design by Cliff Watt in association with
Sundance Publishing

Hoaxes, Fibs, and Fakes
ISBN 0-7910-8428-0

Photo Credits
pp. 6–7 images reproduced with the permission of
Ringling Bros.–Barnum & Bailey Combined Shows, Inc;
pp. 8–9 courtesy of the Historical Society of Cheshire County,
Keene, New Hampshire;
p. 10 New York State Historical Association, Cooperstown;
p. 17 © Michael Curtain;
p. 24 The Kobal Collection/Paramount;
p. 28 photolibrary.com

Table
of Contents

Loveland Public Library
Loveland, Colo. 80537

Is That for Real?

Do you believe everything you see?

If you do—beware. Hoaxers are everywhere!
The word "hoax" is thought to come from
"hocus" in "hocus-pocus." This is a phrase
used by magicians. Like a magician, a hoaxer
tries to trick you into believing things that
aren't real.

A Great Hoaxer

Who was one of the greatest hoaxers of all times? P. T. Barnum! Phineas Taylor (P. T.) Barnum traveled around America in the 1800s with his incredible circus full of strange **exhibits.** Barnum said that his

PT.BARNUM'S GREATEST SHOW ON EARTH & THE GREAT LO

JUMBO THE PRIDE OF THE BRITISH HEART. HER MAJESTY THE QUEEN HER CHILDREN AND GRAND CHILDREN

SANGER'S ROYAL BRITISH MENAGERIE & GRAND INTER
BARNUM, BAILEY & HUTCHINSON, SOLE

exhibits had some of the weirdest things in the world. Some people paid to see his hoaxes because they really believed them. Others didn't believe his hoaxes were true, but they paid to see them anyway.

P. T. Barnum (1810–1891)

Q: What happened when the king's men played a joke on Humpty Dumpty?
A: *He fell for it.*

The Greatest Show

P. T. Barnum wanted everyone to know about his circus. He called it "The Greatest Show on Earth." His railway car always arrived in a town two weeks before the circus. The outside of the railway car was painted with a picture of Barnum and some of the **exotic** creatures in his circus.

BARNUM'S HOAX NO. 1

Exhibit name: The Feejee Mermaid

The claim: She was the corpse of a beautiful young woman with the tail of a fish.

The hoax: She was really part of a monkey and part of a fish sewed together.

Barnum called one of his animals, "the last **mastodon** on earth." The animal was really an elephant named Jumbo.

BARNUM'S HOAX NO. 2

Exhibit name: Joice Heth
The claim: She was 161 years old—the oldest woman in the world.
The hoax: She was only 80 years old when she died (although she was very wrinkly).

...UTION: Staying too long in a bath 'l make you wrinkly, too.

PIGS TAKE OFF!

Pigs were last seen flying over your place!

A Giant Hoax

P. T. Barnum was always on the lookout for a good hoax. When he read that a man named George Hull had "discovered" a giant, he offered Hull $50,000 to buy it. Hull had spent a long time making this fake giant and then burying it. He didn't want to sell it. So Barnum decided to make his own giant. He told the newspapers that Hull's giant was a fake and his was the real one. A double hoax!

Digging up George Hull's giant, October 1869

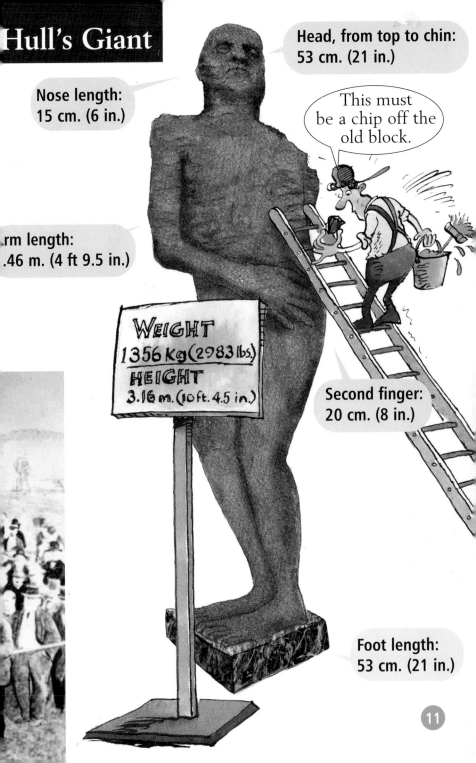

Fooling Around

Warning! Warning! Hoax zone ahead. Watch out for those tricksters . . .

If someone asks you to buy a can of striped paint, a left-handed hammer, or elbow grease, check the date on your calendar.

It's probably April 1—April Fool's Day!

ELBOW GREASE

A Spaghetti Spoof

On April Fool's Day, in 1957, an English TV program showed Swiss farmers picking spaghetti from trees. Hundreds of people called the TV station and asked how to grow spaghetti trees. They were told to place a **sprig** of spaghetti in a can of tomato sauce and hope for the best.

At that time, many people didn't know how spaghetti was made. So they believed that it could grow on trees!

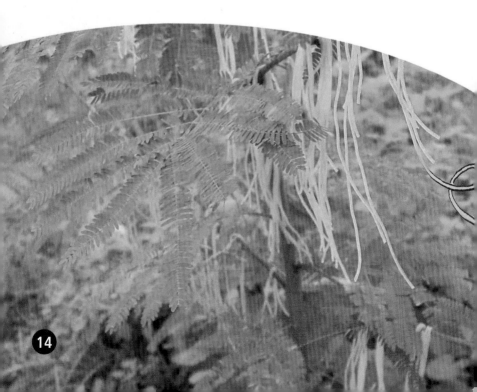

How to Make a Hoax Spaghetti Tree

Cook some spaghetti.

Hang the cooked spaghetti on a tree.

Film the spaghetti tree for the evening news.

Where's the sauce?

Would You Buy It?

On April 1, 1998, an American company advertised a left-handed hamburger for left-handed burger eaters. The new hamburger was supposed to be heavier on the left so the toppings wouldn't spill out on the right. Many people believed the hoax and tried to order the burger.

Sweat A-Weigh
Would you like to lose weight through your feet? On April 1, 2000, a British newspaper claimed you could—with Fatsox. Just sweat the fat into the socks, then wash the fat away. Was this for real? Fat chance!

New Left-Handed Hamburger

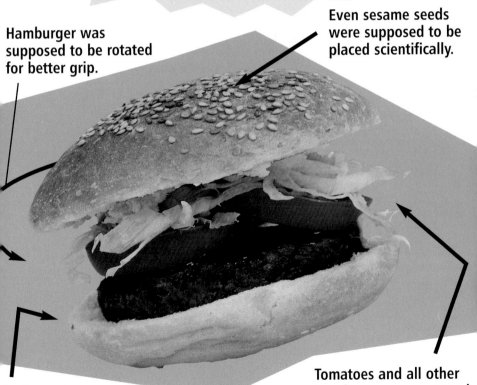

Hamburger was supposed to be rotated for better grip.

Even sesame seeds were supposed to be placed scientifically.

he lower bun was upposed to be adjusted or shift in weight.

Tomatoes and all other toppings were supposed to be rearranged.

Q: Which side of a hamburger is left?
A: *The side that isn't eaten.*

Jumping to Conclusions

We often believe things we read, especially things that sound scientific. On April 1, 1976, **astronomer** Patrick Moore announced that Pluto would pass behind Jupiter. He said that this **alignment**, or lining up, of the planets would affect gravity on Earth. If people jumped in the air at the exact moment the planets were in line, they would be able to float—just like astronauts in space. Some people said they had floated up to the ceiling!

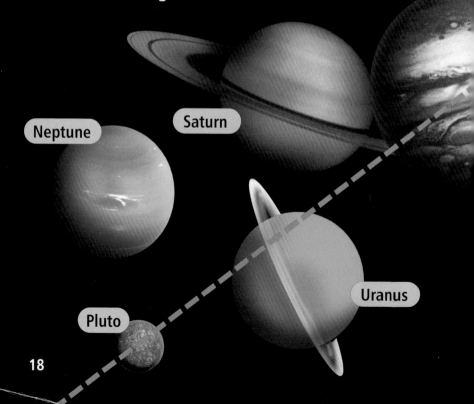

Neptune

Saturn

Uranus

Pluto

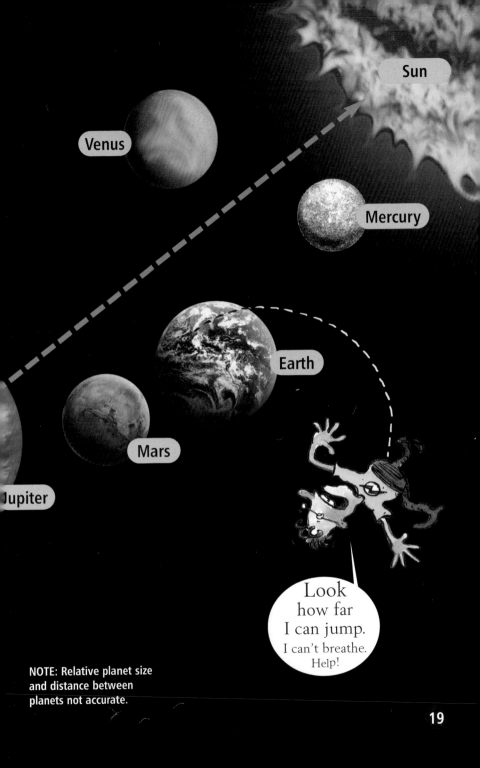

Hot Off the Press

Here's another scientific hoax. On April 1, 1995, a magazine announced that a Dr. Aprile Pazzo had discovered a new creature in the Antarctic— the hotheaded ice borer.

The animal was supposedly named a hotheaded ice borer because it had a hot bone in its forehead. This strange animal used the hot bone to melt the ice around penguins. When a penguin sank into the slush, the ice borers attacked and ate it.

That's enough melting, Arnold. Here comes supper!

Martians and More

Everyone is listening to the radio. Each news bulletin is more terrifying than the last! Aliens have invaded Earth!

Would you believe a radio report that Martians had landed on Earth? Thousands of people did. Some hoaxers use the radio, the newspaper, or photographs to make their hoaxes seem real.

The Day of the Martians

It was 1938. A news bulletin interrupted the music on the radio. There were blue flames on Mars! The music continued. Then there was another bulletin. A **meteor** had fallen in New Jersey! No, it wasn't a meteor.
It was a spaceship—full of Martian soldiers! They were marching. They were armed . . .

People ran into the streets. Some people even panicked.

By that night, most people knew the truth. The world was safe. Actor Orson Welles had been reading H. G. Wells's book *The War of the Worlds* on the radio for Halloween.

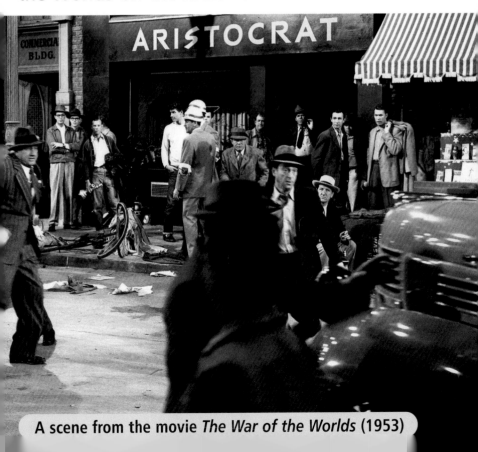

A scene from the movie *The War of the Worlds* (1953)

In 1835—about 100 years before the Martian radio play—people in New York read an amazing story in the *Sun* newspaper. There was life on the moon!

The story said that Sir John Herschel, a famous British astronomer, had invented a powerful telescope. Through it, he could see fantastic things on the moon, including pyramids, blue unicorns, and humanlike creatures with bat wings.

The moon as seen through a normal telescope

Q: What kind of insects live on the moon?
A: *Lunar-ticks.*

For six days, the newspaper published articles about these marvelous discoveries. On the seventh day, the paper announced it was all a hoax.

A close up of the moon as seen through Herschel's telescope

Phoneygraphs

We believe what we see with our own eyes. But sometimes it is best to look at things twice! Hoaxers have produced photographs of aliens, UFOs, and ghosts!

Loch Ness monster photo, by Dr. Wilson

In 1934, Dr. Robert Wilson photographed a long-necked creature in the murky water of Loch Ness, in Scotland. Many people believed that this was one of the first photographs of the Loch Ness monster. What do you think?

Hoax Competition

Are you easily fooled?
Where do you fall on the hoax scale?

Hoax Scale

never
fooled

easily
fooled

If you belong at the "easily fooled" end, send in this entry to win a big prize. See page 64 for details.

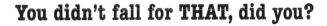

You didn't fall for THAT, did you?

Fact File

One of Barnum's exhibits was called "The Great Unknown." People paid to see it, but when they got inside, they saw . . . NOTHING!

If you read or hear the name Loof Lirpa, be suspicious of whatever comes next! Spell Loof Lirpa backward to see why.

In 1917, two English schoolgirls took fake photographs of themselves dancing with fake pixies. The photos fooled people for years.

Sir Peter Scott gave the Loch Ness monster a scientific name: *Nessiteras Rhombopteryx*. If you rearrange the letters, they spell out: Monster Hoax by Sir Peter S.

Give me an "S"!

Glossary

alignment when two bodies, such as planets, line up

astronomer a scientist who studies stars and planets

exhibits things on display

exotic something from outside the country you live in; foreign

meteor a flaming streak in the sky caused when small pieces of space rock burn up as they pass through Earth's atmosphere

mastodon a large mammal that died out many thousands of years ago

sprig a small piece of a plant with its leaves

Index